W9-AFJ-359

CHICAGO CUBS

STARS, STATS, HISTORY, AND MORE!

BY K. C. KELLEY

childsworld.com

Published by The Child's World®
1980 Lookout Drive • Mankato, MN 56003-1705
800-599-READ • www.childsworld.com

ISBN 9781503828186
LCCN 2018944831

Printed in the United States of America
PAO2392

Photo Credits:
Cover: Joe Robbins (2).
Interior: AP Images: Jeff Roberson 10, Morry Gash 19,
Daniel Bartel/Icon Sportswire 20, Jimmy Simmons/Icon
Sportswire 27. Dreamstime.com: Lawrence Weselowski,
Jr. 13, Ffooter 14, MBr Images 23. Library of Congress: 9.
Joe Robbins: 1, 24. Newscom: Adam Bow/Icon Sportswire
5, Patrick Gorski/Icon Sportswire 6, John J. Kim/TNS 17,
Harry E. Walker/MCT 29.

About the Author

K.C. Kelley is a huge sports
fan who has written more
than 100 books for kids. His
favorite sport is baseball.
He has also written about
football, basketball, soccer,
and even auto racing! He lives
in Santa Barbara, California.

On the Cover
Main photo: third baseman
Kris Bryant
Inset: Hall of Famer Ernie Banks

CONTENTS

GO, CUBS!

For more than 100 years, the Chicago Cubs lost. They lost a lot! They lost year after year. Cubs fans stayed true, though. The team came close to winning a few times, but fell short of the top. Finally, in 2016, the Cubs won the **World Series**! Cubs fans cheered! It was a nice ending to a long story. Today, the Cubs have a solid team. Cubs fans want another trophy. Let's meet the Chicago Cubs!

Left-hander Jon Lester helped the Cubs win the World Series in 2016. ➤

WHO ARE THE CUBS?

The Chicago Cubs play in the National League (NL). That group is part of Major League Baseball (MLB). MLB also includes the American League (AL). There are 30 teams in MLB. The winner of the NL plays the winner of the AL in the World Series. The Cubs won the World Series in 2016. That was their first championship since 1908!

◄ Speedy second baseman Javier Baez slides into home plate. He's safe!

WHERE THEY CAME FROM

The Cubs are one of the oldest teams in baseball. They were part of the NL's first year in 1876. (The team was part of another **pro** league, too. It was in the National Association from 1871 to 75.) "Cubs" is the team's fourth name. From 1876 to 1889, the team name was White Stockings. Then it was the Colts until 1897. For the next five years, the team had the odd name of Orphans. Finally, in 1903, the team's name was changed to Cubs.

Mordecai "Three Finger" Brown played for the Cubs from ➤
1904 to 1912. He helped them win two World Series.

BROWN Chicago Nat'l

WHO THEY PLAY

The Cubs play 162 games in a season. That's a lot of baseball! They play most of their games against other NL teams. The Cubs are part of the NL Central Division. The other NL Central teams are the Cincinnati Reds, the Milwaukee Brewers, the Pittsburgh Pirates, and the St. Louis Cardinals. The Cubs and Cardinals are big **rivals**!

◄ *Tommy La Stella of the Cubs grabs the ball. He is about to tag out Jedd Gyorko of the rival Cardinals.*

WHERE THEY PLAY

The Cubs play at Wrigley Field. It opened in 1914. It is the oldest ballpark in the NL! Few ballparks are more famous than the "Friendly Confines." Wrigley's outfield walls are made of brick. Ivy vines grow on the walls. For decades, every game there was played during the day. Finally, Wrigley got lights in 1988. The Cubs could finally play nighttime games at Wrigley!

Baseballs sometimes get lost in the famous ➤
ivy on the Wrigley Field walls.

THE BASEBALL FIELD

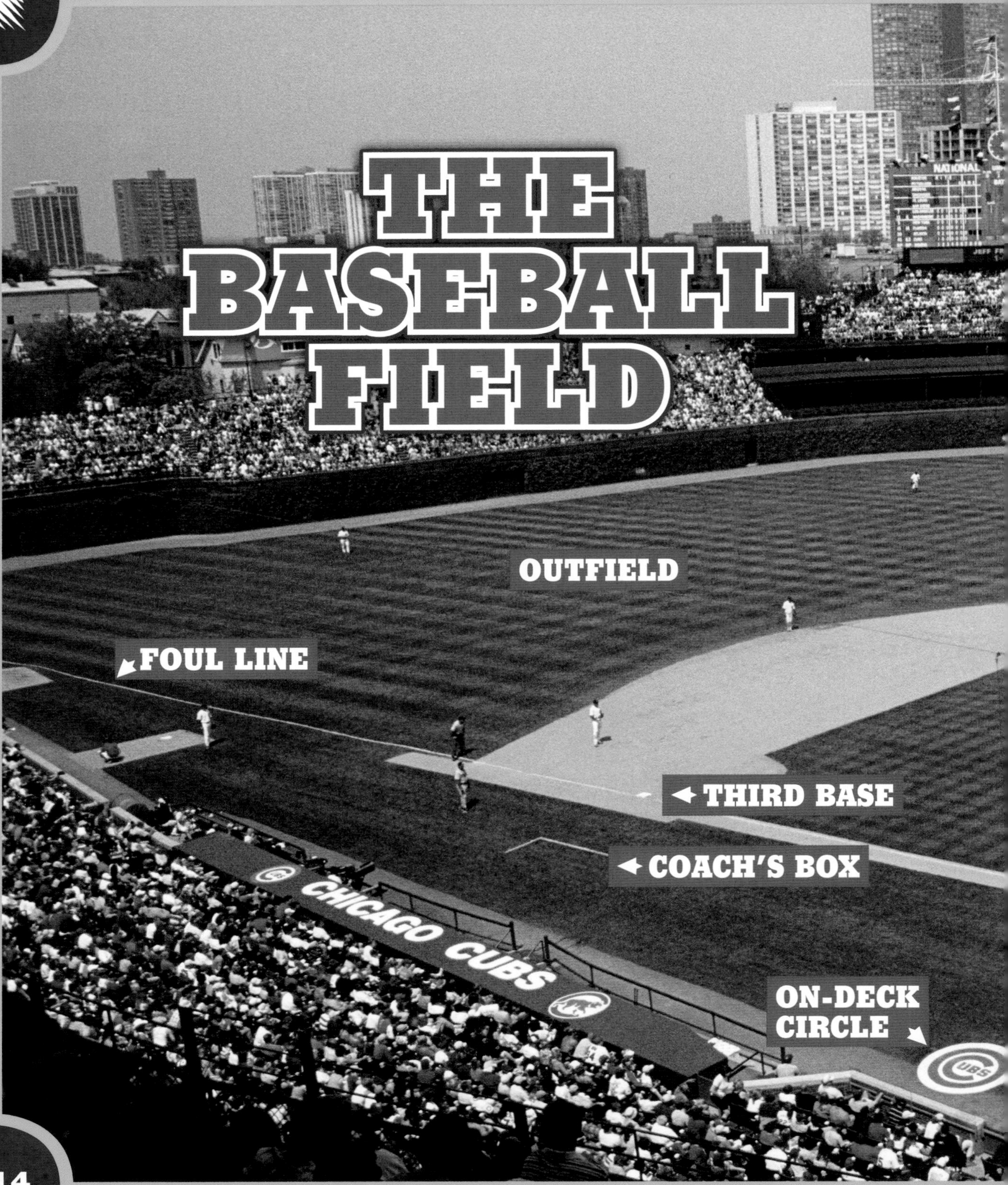

OUTFIELD

FOUL LINE

◄ THIRD BASE

◄ COACH'S BOX

ON-DECK
CIRCLE ↘

CHICAGO CUBS

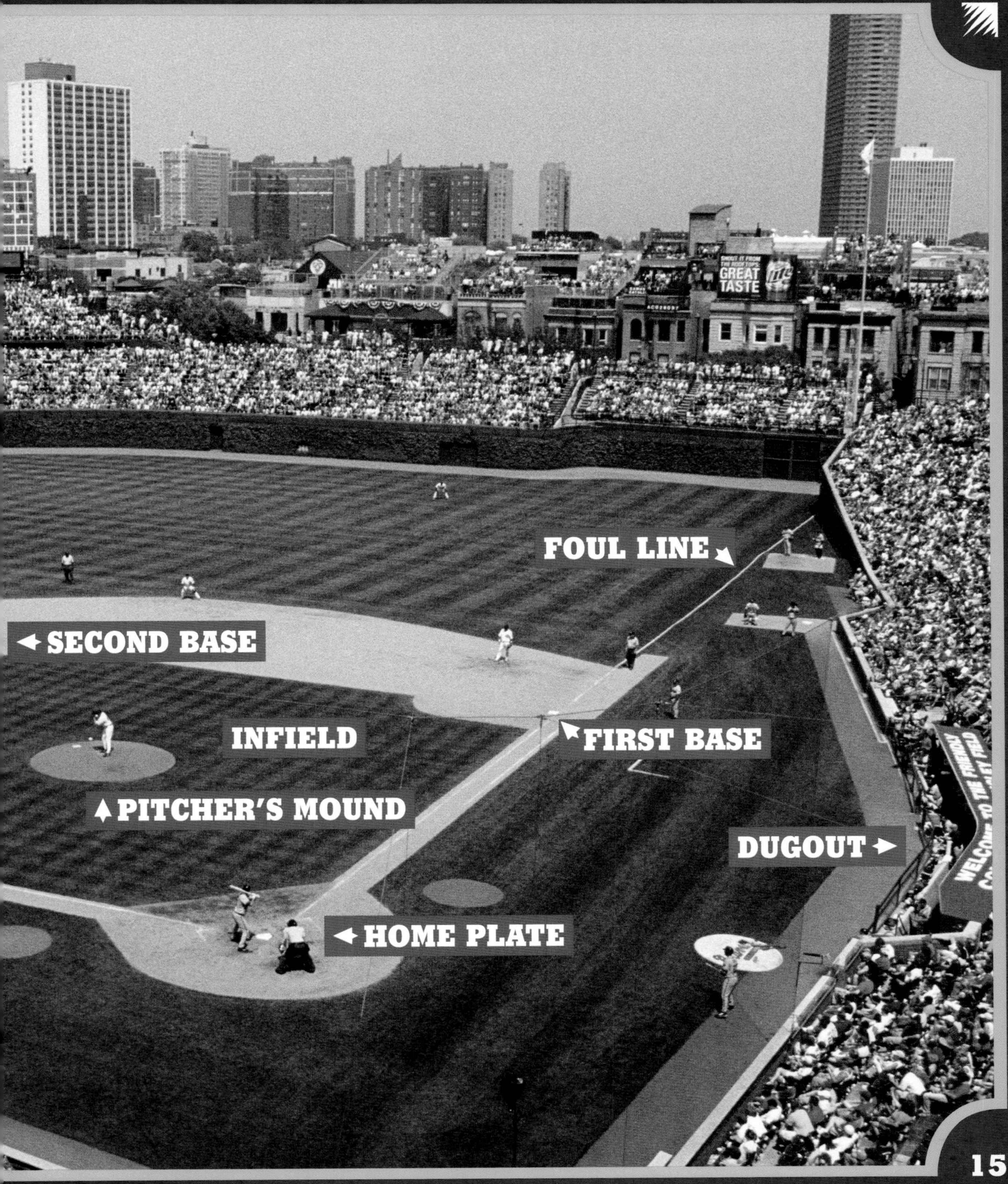

FOUL LINE

SECOND BASE

INFIELD

FIRST BASE

PITCHER'S MOUND

DUGOUT

HOME PLATE

BIG DAYS

The Cubs have played for more than a century. In that time, they have had many memorable seasons and games. Here's a look at some of the most famous.

1907 and 1908—This was a great time to be a Cubs' fan. The team won two World Series in a row! In 1907, they beat the Detroit Tigers. The Cubs pitchers allowed only six runs in five games. In 1908, the Cubs beat the Tigers again.

1958 and 59—Shortstop Ernie Banks was named the NL **Most Valuable Player** (MVP) both years.

As an Indians player walks off, the Cubs celebrated ➤
their 2016 World Series championship.

2016—Finally, after 108 years, the Cubs won it all. They won the final two games of the series over the Cleveland Indians. Then they brought the trophy back to Chicago!

TOUGH DAYS

Every season can't end with a title. Here's a look back at some games and seasons Cubs fans might want to forget!

1969—This was a year to forget. The Cubs played in the NL East Division back then. On September 2, they led the East by five games. Then they lost their next eight games in a row! They finished in second place . . . again.

1984—The Cubs won the first two games of the **NL Championship Series** (NLCS). One more win would send the Cubs to the World Series. Then the Cubs lost three games in a row and went home.

2003—The Cubs made the NLCS again. They led the Florida Marlins in Game 6. The World Series was just a few outs away. Then a fan reached out of the stands. He accidentally knocked the ball away from a Cubs fielder. The Marlins rallied to win the game and the NLCS. It was another sad day for the Cubbies.

▲ *The fan in the blue hat knocked the ball away from a Cubs fielder. The mistake gave the Marlins a chance to win.*

MEET THE FANS!

Cubs fans are loyal! They stuck with their losing team for many years. When the team finally won, the fans were overjoyed! Cubs fans wave a white "W" flag when the team wins. Fans in the outfield throw back any home run ball that was hit by an opponent. Some fans even sit on rooftops outside the ballpark! It's a different way to watch their favorite team.

◄ *The "Bleacher Creatures" fill Wrigley Field. They love waving "W" flags after wins by their favorite team.*

HEROES THEN

The Cubs have not had many championships. They have had a lot of great players, though. When he was a kid, Mordecai Brown had an accident on a farm. He hurt his hand. It gave him a famous nickname: Three Finger Brown. It didn't stop him from being a great pitcher! Ernie Banks was known as "Mr. Cub." He was a slugging shortstop and first baseman. He always had a positive attitude and a big smile. Ryne Sandberg was a ten-time All-Star at second base. "Ryno" was the 1984 NL MVP.

Ernie Banks starred for the Cubs from 1953 to 1970. ➤
He was elected to the Baseball Hall of Fame in 1977.

HEROES NOW

Kris Bryant and Anthony Rizzo are a pair of Cubs sluggers. Bryant plays third base. Rizzo is across the diamond at first base. They both smash homers over the ivy in Wrigley Field. Jon Lester is a **veteran** pitcher. He came over from the Red Sox and helped the Cubs win it all in 2016. Catcher Willson Contreras helps out on defense and with his bat.

◄ *Kris Bryant was the NL Rookie of the Year in 2015. The next year, he was named the NL MVP!*

GEARING UP

Baseball players wear team uniforms. On defense, they wear leather gloves to catch the ball. As batters, they wear hard helmets. This protects them from pitches. Batters hit the ball with long wood bats. Each player chooses his own size of bat. Catchers have the toughest job. They wear a lot of protection.

THE BASEBALL

The outside of the Major League baseball is made from cow leather. Two leather pieces shaped like 8's are stitched together. There are 108 stitches of red thread. These stitches help players grip the ball. Inside, the ball has a small center of cork and rubber. Hundreds of feet of yarn are tightly wound around this center.

← CATCHER'S MASK AND HELMET

CHEST PROTECTOR →

WRIST BANDS →

← CATCHER'S MITT

SHIN GUARDS →

CATCHER'S GEAR

TEAM STATS

Here are some of the all-time career records for the Chicago Cubs. All these stats are through the 2018 regular season.

HOME RUNS	
Sammy Sosa	545
Ernie Banks	512

RBI	
Cap Anson	1,880
Ernie Banks	1,636

BATTING AVERAGE	
Bill Madlock	.336
Riggs Stephenson	.336

STOLEN BASES	
Frank Chance	402
Bill Lange	400

WINS	
Charlie Root	201
Mordecai Brown	188

SAVES	
Lee Smith	180
Bruce Sutter	133

Hard-throwing Carlos Zambrano was a Cub from 2001 to 2011. ➤

STRIKEOUTS

Fergie Jenkins	2,038
Carlos Zambrano	1,542

GLOSSARY

Most Valuable Player (MOHST VALL-you-uh-bull PLAY-ur) an award given each year by the AL and NL to the top player

NL Championship Series (ENN-ELL CHAMP-ee-un-ship SEE-reez) a best-of-seven set of games after the season; the winner reaches the World Series

playoffs (PLAY-offs) games played between top teams to determine who moves ahead

pro (PROH) an athlete who is paid to play a sport

rivals (RYE-vulls) two people or groups competing for the same thing

shortstop (SHORT-stahp) a baseball position that stands between second base and third base

veteran (VET-er-un) an athlete with several years of experience

World Series (WURLD SEE-reez) the championship of Major League Baseball, played between the winners of the AL and NL

FIND OUT MORE

IN THE LIBRARY

Connery-Boyd, Peg. *Chicago Cubs 2016 World Series Champions: Big Book of Activities.* Chicago: Sourcebooks/Jabberwocky, 2017.

Fishman, Jon M. *Kris Bryant (Sports All-Stars).* Minneapolis, MN: Lerner Books, 2018.

Herzog, Brad. *W Is for Wrigley: The Friendly Confines Alphabet.* Ann Arbor, MI: Sleeping Bear Press, 2013.

ON THE WEB

Visit our Web site for links about the Chicago Cubs:
childsworld.com/links

Note to Parents, Teachers, and Librarians: We routinely verify our Web links to make sure they are safe and active sites. So encourage your readers to check them out!

#